The Harp of God 24

The Harp of God 24

David Castillo

Library of Congress Control Number:		2014910289
ISBN:	Softcover	978-1-4633-8598-9
	eBook	978-1-4633-8597-2

This book was printed in the United States of America.

Rev. date: 17/07/2014

To order additional copies of this book, please contact:
Palibrio LLC
1663 Liberty Drive
Suite 200
Bloomington, IN 47403
Toll Free from the U.S.A 877.407.5847
Toll Free from Mexico 01.800.288.2243
Toll Free from Spain 900.866.949
From other International locations +1.812.671.9757
Fax: 01.812.355.1576
orders@palibrio.com
635801

CONTENTS

INTRODUCTION

I, David, was in the world without knowing about the salvation that God gives in the forgiveness of sins. In Brawley C.A. with the prayers of a Christian group, I received the Lord Jesus as my only savior asking for God's forgiveness I became a Christian since January of 2005. Just a couple days after I accepted our Lord Jesus as my only savior, I was walking at the north-west side of Brawley which is Westmorland C.A. I was alone facing the sky and talking to the Lord Jesus, at that night I have a spiritual experience, the Holy Spirit came on me, and as I overjoyed of his grace facing the sky I feel his voice (with no sound) together with the bits of my heart saying; "comeback" I heard it four times, and as I tried to speak not understanding what really was meaning, the holy spirit leaded me to the ground that I couldn't move and the grace of the Lord was stronger over me, I was feeling his voice (with no sound) together with the bits of my heart saying the same words another four times; "come back" and as I could I responded Him that I will, at that very moment all of it disappear like if it was slowly dissolving from me. I admit that I did not understand what the Lord Jesus Christ was meaning to tell me, but I must say that from that very moment my life drastically changed, I was not a biblical reader, reading or writing was not my ability, but I became one as I learned to be a true Christian, but still did not understood the true meaning of God's words, and years came to pass, the world was not the same to me, it became worst, but I grew in the faith stronger and stronger. In November of 2008 I moved from Richmond V.A. to Raleigh N.C. after many days I met a Christian family, I was in love with them but I knew that I couldn't stay longer for I'd have more enemies than friends, something difficult to explain but easy to understand, at that time I was down in faith and losing hope before I met them, now they are an important part in my life even though I couldn't tell them how much I loved them I know they will know this someday, while I was with them in their church they convinced me to be baptized in order to completely be in God's word and in his love! In the name of the Lord it was done, just before I leave Raleigh N.C. and I leave with no chance to say goodbye but I am thankful to them. As years came to pass I found my purpose, as a believer I'd have pass so many test in the word of God, I believed in a glorious day, and I have forgotten my enemies and asking for the forgiveness of my God, everywhere I go I carry on this purpose, I genteelly fight against the unbelievers with the sword of God, and I defeated them with the only purpose to lead them to see the truth, but the message is not about my life at all, just let you know that I am here for you. I've lost most of me and so many doors were closed to me by carry on my testimony that God gave me to give to his holy church, I've being test by the Lord's will, but because everything is ready, this is my testimony that I must finish in the name of Jesus Christ of Nazareth; "three days and one night" amen! Dedicated to my holy family in Jesus Christ, from Abraham to everyone in this last days, be blessed and the grace of the Lord be with you all, this is my only wish, and as peter say, "Silver or gold I do not have, but what I do have I give you".

CHAPTER 01

"THE LITTLE SCROLL"

Do not be deceived, anyone who speak about prophesy and about God, shall acknowledge the Lord Jesus as our only savior, he who prophesy shall understand the Jewish feasts and the signs of heaven above, for this signs comes from God's commandments, he who preach shall understand what he is preaching about, and who he is serving. If they don't have an own understanding and clearly who they are serving and what they are preaching about, the love for their brothers and sisters shall be enough only in the name of the Lord, because even the love for our enemies comes from God as he commanded us. Out of the Holy Scriptures the testimony is valuable if there is no lie on their mouths about what they preach about and who they served, the testimony doesn't have nothing to do with the law of this world, a law beaker is the one who brakes the commandments of God such as the sixth commandment, "You shall not killed". In fact we live by faith and we are saved by the blood of the Lamb. Give to that nation what belongs to them, and give to God what belongs to Him. At the end of times you will understand what I am trying to tell you, but for now is a test, so you may take the choice to love this world or leave it in victory through The Lord's Blood.

Mark 12:[17] *Then Jesus said to them,* **"Give back to Caesar what is Caesar's and to God what is God's."**

The blood of the lamb cleans us from all our sins, accepting him as our only savior, and cleaning our robes from our sins and making them white as linen, in fact we live by faith.

The first commandment is about not having other god but the Lord God Almighty, for there is no other god in this life nor in the coming life, the forgiveness of all this sin comes from God by never repeating this sin ever again, with the proper repentance and baptism in his name.

The second commandment is about not worshiping idols made of wood or stone in the figure of something or anything above the earth or under the sky or under the sea. The forgiveness of all this sin comes from God by never repeating this sin ever again, with the proper repentance and baptism in his name.

The third commandment is about the ones who make promises or prophesy events that doesn't comes from the Lord and so misuses the name of the Lord for gain purposes. The forgiveness of all this sin comes from God by never repeating this sin ever again, with the proper repentance and baptism in his name.

The fourth commandment is about not to forget the seven days of creation, starting with Sunday and working only six days on the seven days week, not forgetting why the seven day is for rest, and why God did made the Sabbath day holy(God did made Sabbath day holy for a very important reasons). The forgiveness of all this sin comes from God by remembering the holy commandments such as the Sabbath day, with the proper repentance and with baptism in his name.

The fifth commandment is about honoring father and mother as well, the forgiveness of all this sin comes from God by never repeating this sin ever again, with the proper repentance and in baptism in his name.

The sixth commandment is about not eating flesh, and not eating dust, and not to kill, the punishment over the murder is to be death by the same sword he murdered, but God's forgiveness is not simple because this sin is serious. From God the forgiveness is based of justice and his own authority to forgive this sin is by the intentions of the heart, only God can judged and forgive, in the Holy Scriptures Moses was found worthy to guide Israel out of Egypt by God's command even he was forgiven like all sin erased from his life. For those, never repeat this sin ever again, with the proper repentance and baptism in his name, may the Lord fine grace in you, and so you be saved from his wrath that is coming as great punishment over the earth and mankind.

The seventh seal is about adultery, the forgiveness of all this sin comes from God by never repeating this sin ever again, remember Mary Magdalene and the compassion of the Lord, now with the proper repentance and baptism in his name, be saved.

The eight commandment is about not to steal, the forgiveness of all this sin comes from God by never repeating this sin ever again, with the proper repentance and in baptism in his name.

The nine commandment is about not to give false testimony against your neighbor, this refer the evil accusation against the oppressed by false witnesses and false accusations, and this is how its written in the Holy Scriptures, the lie becomes a great sin when the accusation is based on lies made by the own authority of man for gain purposes. The forgiveness of all this sin comes from God by never repeating this sin ever again, with the proper repentance and in baptism in his name each one by himself.

The ten commandment is about the desired of someone's possessions such as his wife, or someone's husband, or his home, or his wealth, or any possession that anyone could have to be desired by others, this sin becomes great to be judged as an abomination to God, for the Lord will not hold innocent the one who does not repent of all these sins. The forgiveness of all this sin comes from God by never repeating this sin ever again, with the proper repentance and in baptism in his name.

Now before I can begin to teach you by the grace of the will of the Lord that is over me as an instrument sounds beautifully, I must explain this to you, his words sounds through the Holy Scriptures and sweet on my lips as I preach and glorified his name, his words must be in yours, and may you not understand me clearly, but I am here to stop you from going in the wrong way because you are going to see an end, you must listen to be prepared, and you shall stand, the Lord will guide you and I will prepared the way for you, so the message will be sounding like a trumpet that everyone will hear, I am with you, I am for you, and the Lord choose me to be born to guide you in his name, you may also not understand this words I am saying, but at the end of this little book you will understand why this is called "the little scroll" and so, you will wait with me for our savior and God. I am not here to judge no one, I am just here to keep you from doing the greatest mistake of lifetime.

Exodus 20: [20] *Moses said to the people,* **"Do not be afraid. God has come to test you, so that the fear of God will be with you to keep you from sinning."**

Now Brothers and Sisters we have to be prepared for prophesy will come to end. Everything in a single day will be changed and the elements will be melted and the earth will have a new point of view, everything that makes peoples' life such any possessions will disappear, there will be a day when you shall understand that everything will have to stay here, to be made new through fire, do not love the things in the world, love the lights over the world, because like a star for ever and ever you must choose to be with your holy family, our holy family. The end will come, and the present world will end, a new earth will be found. But the word of God lives in each one of us, for God's word came from heaven as rain waters on the earth and we are his plants and trees of good seed, this is his garden, "The Holy City". Believe in a glorious day and believe in your God, our God and only savior, Amen.

CHAPTER 02

THESE ARE THE SIX DAYS OF CREATION FROM THE BEGINNING UNTIL THE END OF THE AGE

It's true that the Spirit of God created the heavens in the first four days of creation and as the sun lighted the earth, the plants grew. Then he created the seas and all the sea creatures by the fifth day of creation. Then he created all the leaving on the earth and the creatures that move along the ground and the birds that can fly in the sky, even mankind, all of it by the sixth day of creation. Now this age can be represented as the seventh day of creation when male and female are getting ready for a new home in eternity.

We, by faith, believed that the universe was created at God's command which is God's word, and we have his word, this is light in each one of us, and so by faith we must understand that he created all of us by love, male and female, we are created not just to be saved, but to save and show that we are worthy of God's love and eternal peace from him. But now, I will show you the desire that you have in your heart and mind, this is the true representation by faith and concerns the salvation of the world.

The first day of the week just like the first day of creation, is **"Sunday"**, this very day is of great importance prophetically, symbolically and spiritually, because all the books refer this very day as the beginning of creation. Spiritually, Sunday was the third day when the temple of the Lord was rebuild which is the Lord's body, when he was risen from the death. Jesus Christ is the beginning but six days of creation, like six days of God's work, are based in only one day; **"Sunday"**.

But the first day of creation counts when the Holy Spirit came on Mary, a virgin, and the power of the Most High overshadowed her, and so, the Holy one was to be born and named Jesus, Jesus Christ was born to be called "The son of God" that's why we are sons and daughters of God, both, created by him, for Jesus is the word, and the word was God, the word (God) became flesh, and his twelve apostles knew their Lord and God when he was risen from the grave by his own authority, for when the Jews asked to Jesus for a sign to prove his authority over the temple, he answered to them this about his body (his temple) as a sign of his authority;

*John 2:19 Jesus answered them, "Destroy this temple, **and I will raise it again** in three days."*

John 2:21 **But the temple he had spoken of was his body.**

When you get to the clear understanding of the Holy Scriptures, you clearly understand that Jesus Christ is both, Lord and messiah, and that he is the only one who can rise us at the last day.

This is a little complicated to understand, I know, but just keep in mind this, and stored up his words in your heart, Jesus Christ is the beginning as **"Sunday"**; the day of our Lord's victory over death. And Jesus is the end like Sabbath day; the day of our God's coming to make the final judgment over the evil and salvation to his Holy people.

The beginning of the creation is the first Day of the week which is "Sunday" This very day is to take a very important consideration, for in the book of genesis the four days of creation are based in four days of separations and two days of creation which are in total six days of God's work and all the six days are based in one day; "Sunday".

The four of the six days refer the separation of light from darkness in four representations, like the first separation of light from darkness, the second separation of the waters below from the waters above, the third separation of the earth (trees and plants) from the seas, the fourth separation of the day with the sun, from the night with the moon and stars.

Genesis 1:[3] **And God said, "Let there be light," and there was light.** [4] *God saw that the light was good, and he separated the light from the darkness.* [5] *God called the light "day," and the darkness he called "night." And there was evening, and there was morning—**the first day.***

Matthew 4: [14] **"You are the light of the world.** *A town built on a hill cannot be hidden.* [15] *Neither do people light a lamp and put it under a bowl. Instead they put it on its stand, and it gives light to everyone in the house.* [16] *In the same way,* **let your light shine before others**, *that they may see your good deeds and glorify your Father in heaven.*

Then the fifth day and the sixth day refer the creation of all the leaving and mankind. The fifth day is the creation of all the leaving creatures in the seas—everything that has the breath of life in it—**and this refer spiritual food.**

The sixth day of creation is the last day of God's work, and each one of the six days in God's work, which is creation, are just repeated representations of the day of creation by the command of God's word, but "Sunday" is the climax of the six days of God's word. In creation the Father is the creator of mankind, male and female. God, our heavenly father did send his sons to the world, loving them as if they were just his only one son, and it is written that the great commission is also the word that commands creation after separation by his word;

Matthew 28:[18] ***Then Jesus came to them and said, "All authority in heaven and on earth has been given to me.*** [19] ***Therefore go and make disciples of all nations, baptizing them in the name of the Father and of the Son and of the Holy Spirit,*** [20] ***and teaching them to obey everything I have commanded you. And surely I am with you always, to the very end of the age."***

And to God, our Heavenly Father, we are his only and begotten son for we are loved by him with no exception, he gave his life as an example of true love, just as it's perfectly written by the apostle;

John chapter 15:[13] **Greater love has no one than this: to lay down one's life for one's friends.** *for there is not greater love than laid down one's life.*

This is why we are here, God so loved the world that he did send us to the world to preach everything he has given us to give;

*"John 3:16 For God so loved the world that **he gave his one and only Son, that whoever believes in him shall not perish but have eternal life.** 17 **For God did not send his Son into the world to condemn the world, but to save the world through him.**"*

This is how we received authority from God, with the only purposed to take care of his garden, of his sheep, of his fish, of his sons and daughters, and so our brothers and sister to guide them to the tree of life for salvation and eternal life as a gift from God to the righteous and humble heart who acknowledge him and his love for all of us.

Chapter 03

SABBATH

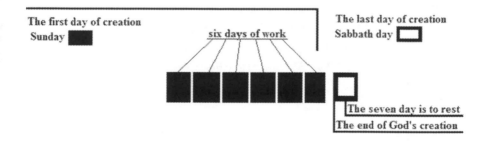

Creation was done by his victory over flesh, this is why it's written so long ago in the Holy Scriptures like if creation was already done, even if creation was in process, the beginning and the end was already given to understand by God's words through his prophets and even he himself teaching humanity in order to protect them.

There are six days of God's creation, like the six days of God's work, but the first day of creation, "Sunday" refer the six days as well.

Here is the sign of the great day of the Lord, the last day when God finished his work of creation. The sign is **"Sabbath day"**.

Genesis 2:[1] Thus the heavens and the earth were completed in all their vast array.

[2] By the seventh day God had finished the work he had been doing; so on the seventh day he rested from all his work.

The Lord did made Saturday a holy day for his Holy people by his victory over death, and our victory at his coming, just as he promised in visions, at his coming we together as if we were "his only son" we will sit at his right side and so stand at his right sight, there in his throne, in heaven, for it is written:

Acts 7:[55] *But Stephen, full of the Holy Spirit, looked up to heaven and saw the glory of God and Jesus standing at the right hand of God.* [56] *"Look", he said, "I see heaven open and* **the son of man standing at the right hand of God.**

Because we are his temple and his throne is in our hearts, we are the church and we represent him, for we are made in his own lightness. And even though it's complicated to understand the vision that refer God's coming it's remarkable and every eye will see him, and so this vision shall be fulfilled.

Genesis 2:[3] **Then God blessed the seventh day and made it holy, because on it he rested from all the work of creating that he had done.**

Because God had finish his creation at the seventh day so God did made holy the Sabbath, because what shall be done was written as done before it started, and what is about to end was written before its beginning.

Before the end, everything is already written, and now the beginning it's gone, as time goes on and it's about to end.

Now Brothers and Sisters we have to be prepared for prophesy will come to end. But the word lives in each one of us, for God's word came from heaven as rain waters on the earth, and just like rain does not return from the ground empty, so you, for you've had received God's word and believe in him, then you came from heaven and you shall not return alone from the dust, because his word came from heaven and lives in you, it will take you where it came from, which is where you belong, believe in a glorious day, and receive the Holy Spirit which is also the understanding of his word;

John 20: [21] *Again Jesus said, "Peace be with you! As the Father has sent me, I am sending you."* [22] **And with that he breathed on them and said, "Receive the Holy Spirit.**

And in this way we understand that the Holy Scriptures were fulfilled just as it is written in the book of Genesis, it is fulfilled:

Genesis 2: [7] **Then the LORD God formed a man from the dust of the ground and breathed into his nostrils the breath of life, and the man became a living being.**

Genesis 2: [15] *The LORD God took the man and put him in the Garden of Eden* **to work it and take care of it.**

The fruit of the tree of knowledge of good and evil is based in not taking someone's life, like eating human flesh, which is also eating dust, and the one who kill by sword shall be killed by the sword. In the same way all of this refer the sixth commandment of the ten written in the law of mosses by God's word;

Exodus 20: [13] **"You shall not murder.**

Genesis 2:[17] **but you must not eat from the tree of the knowledge of good and evil,** *for when you eat from it you will certainly die."*

In the middle of the Garden which is the Holy City, was the tree of life and the tree of knowledge of good and evil. The tree of the knowledge of good and evil is the Lamb and his 12 apostles also figuratively called 12 fruits, this is the beginning also called "Sunday".

Also in the middle of the garden was the tree of life and his 12 fruits of eternal life, this refer God's coming and his holy ones with him, this is the end also called **"Sabbath"**.

Revelation 7:[17] **For the Lamb at the center of the throne** *will be their shepherd; 'he will lead them to springs of living water.'* **'And God will wipe away every tear from their eyes.'"**

When you have a clear understanding of the Holy Scriptures, you come to understand that **the Lamb is the Lord God Almighty**, by the way creation was placed and written by him who is the author of life, and there is no division between the Spirit of God in the foundation of the world. And then the Son of God in the beginning of creation as the tree of the knowledge of good and evil with twelve fruits and with the sign of the beginning "Sunday". And at the end of creation, God, our heavenly father is like a tree of eternal life, as the Sabbath day sign is disclosed.

Revelation 21:[22] *I did not see a temple in the city, because* **the Lord God Almighty** *and* **the Lamb are its temple.**

In conclusion on this chapter, Sunday is the beginning and **Sabbath day,** this day is Saturday and **is the end of the age and the end of God's creation as well.**

CHAPTER 04

THE TEMPLE OF THE LORD

Now, we now by faith, that Sunday is the first day of creation and it's the day of the beginning, also discloses the last day of creation that is Sabbath and the end of the age.

Now, we are going to focus on Sunday, it's prophetically, spiritually and even symbolically called the beginning of creation, because this very day was the Lord's victory over flesh. But it has two representations, one it's about the third day that is Sunday, and refer the temple like the body of Jesus Christ, and it's very important to keep in mind how this prophetic speech was written in the book of the prophet Haggai, symbolically pointing the 24th day to take great consideration, because the 24th day is symbolic and refer also the Sunday, so this is the sign that Jesus Christ gave to the people at the temple area in Jerusalem:

John 2: [19] **Jesus answered them, "Destroy this temple, and I will raise it again in three days."**

It's remarkable the words "I will raise it again" but we are on the sign of the third day, which you already know the third day was Sunday, the day when the Lord rebuild the temple, and yes, it took three days;

John 2:[21] **But the temple he had spoken of was his body.**

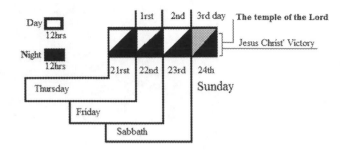

The 21rst day

Now, the first year of Darius the mede, and the second year of Darius the mede are symbolic, written in the Holy scriptures like the Glory of the Lord which is the temple but is talking about Jesus' body, and the Holy Scriptures were fulfil as it's written in the book of the prophet Haggai:

Haggai 2:9 'The glory of this present house will be greater than the glory of the former house,' says the LORD Almighty…

And it's very important to keep in mind how this prophetic speech was written in the book of the prophet Haggai, symbolically pointing the 24th day to take great consideration, because the 24th day is symbolic and refer also the Sunday, **Sunday was the third day by the sign of the temple of the Lord, but Sunday was also symbolically called "The 24th day" by the book of the prophet Haggai. On the book of Haggai is also pointed the 21rst day. These days are based by its figurative meaning of four days, those are; the 21rst day that was on Thursday, the 22nd day that was on Friday, the 23rd day that was on Sabbath, on those days the 24th day was on Sunday, early that day Jesus rose from the grave:**

Haggai 2:1 On the twenty-first day of the seventh month, the word of the LORD came through the prophet Haggai:

Jesus Christ suffered death for our salvation, to be fulfil was very necessary, this is called the first glory of the house of the Lord, and the 21rst day which was on Thursday, this day is knowing as the last supper also when Judas Iscariot betrayed Jesus Christ for thirty silver coins, Just like it's written in the Holy Scriptures by the prophet

Daniel by God's will, when the chief priests *gave to Judas Iscariot thirty silver coins and so Judas Iscariot betrayed Jesus on that day*:

Daniel 10: [13] **But the prince of the kingdom of Persia withstood me twenty-one days;** *but, behold, Michael, one of the chief princes, came to help me: because I was detained there with the king of Persia.*

The 21ˢᵗ day was on Thursday, four days before Sunday, and Sunday was on the 24ᵗʰ Day. The 21ˢᵗ day also refer the first year of Darius the mede. Now the Lord is symbolically represented in the book of Daniel as Gabriel and this is for the signs of the first day of creation, Michael is the Lord's helper on the signs of the first day of creation, but the vision concerns the last days, in the last days Michael gives the seal of the living God before the end of the age, but the 21rst day is written in the beginning, just as it is written in the book of the prophet Daniel, written about the 21rst day that it was on Thursday;

Daniel 11:[11] *"As for me, in* **the first** *year of Darius the Mede, I stood up to confirm and strengthen him.*

The 24ᵗʰ day

The 24ᵗʰ day refer **the second glory** of the hose of the Lord also known as Jesus' body, which in this present day is known as Sunday;

Haggai 2:[10] **On the twenty-fourth day** *of the ninth month, in* **the second** *year of Darius,* *the word of the* LORD *came to the prophet Haggai:*

In the book of the prophet Haggai is remarkable how is pointing **the 24ᵗʰ day** to give a careful thought, its speaking about the Lord's temple which we know it's symbolic meaning, it's Jesus' body.

Haggai 2:[18] '*From this day on, from this* **twenty-fourth day** *of the ninth month, give careful thought to* **the day** *when the foundation of* **the** LORD'***s temple** *was laid. Give careful thought:*

Haggai 2:[19] *Is there yet any seed left in the barn? Until now, the vine and the fig tree, the pomegranate and the olive tree have not borne fruit.* **"'From this day on I will bless you.'"**

This 24th was when Jesus rose early that day on Sunday, which is **the first** day of the week and that is the reason why it has many representations, like, our **first** love, **the beginning** of creation, and **the 24th day** is also the day when the Lord make all things **new**, the **new** Jerusalem, this is also **the new** song, and in creation as you know by faith, **the new** heaven and **new earth**, and the **24th day**, And because God pointed the 24th day as the seal of the living God then we are symbolically called **"The signet ring of the Lord Almighty"** the Lord's temple in the book of the prophet Haggai is fulfilled:

*Haggai 2:23 "'**On that day**,' declares the* LORD *Almighty, 'I will take you, my servant Zerubbabel son of Shealtiel,' declares the* LORD, *'and **I will make you like my signet ring**, for I have chosen you,' declares the* LORD *Almighty."*

The 24th day is Sunday and is the seal of the living God for it represent the six days of creation (144,000) but the six day of God's work in creation are based only in one day that is **"Sunday" (24)** we are like the signet ring of God Almighty understanding the name of our heavenly father because he is worthy, and so disclosing to mankind the day that God took away our sins by his blood, is like putting on their foreheads the seal of the leaving God before the end of the age comes and God's wrath as well. For this reason we must be baptized in repentance and dressed in Holy water as we hold to his promise of the crown of life and eternal peace as well.

THURSDAY, FRIDAY, SATURDAY AND SUNDAY.

The 21rst day refer Thursday (The Lamb of God)

On Thursday was the last supper, when Jesus Christ have dinner with his twelve apostles, *the day of Unleavened Bread on which the Passover Lamb had to be sacrificed. That same day, Judas Iscariot betrayed him.*

*Mark 22:7 Then came the day of Unleavened Bread on which **the Passover Lamb had to be sacrificed.***

Matthew 26: ₃₁ *Then Jesus told them,* **"This very night** *you will all fall away on account of me, for it is written: "I will strike the shepherd, and the sheep of the flock will be scattered.'*

The 22ⁿᵈ day refer Friday

On Friday, Jesus was put to death by his brothers (spiritual speech), he was the verb and the verb was with God, even though the verb was God, this express the integrity of time, Jesus was meant to overcome before he was born, that's the reason why God was with the verb in the beginning, planning our salvation trough his prophets and saints before the beginning. For now this is Friday, the 22ⁿᵈ day, when his blood cleans us from our sins, there's no greater love than this, inexplicable because it was the creator's desired to be sacrifice for our salvation, his blood, was forgiveness of our sins and the cost was exceeding great.

Mark 15:₃₃ **At noon, darkness came over the whole land until three in the afternoon.**³⁴ **And at three in the afternoon Jesus cried out in a loud voice,** *"Eloi, Eloi, le, and the masabachthani?" (Which means "My God, my God, why have you forsaken me?").*

The 23ʳᵈ day refer Sabbath day

On Sabbath day, the Pharisees asked Pilate to make secured the tomb of Jesus, and Pilate agreed to do as they asked him to order.

Matthew 27:⁶² **The next day, the one after Preparation Day,** *the chief priests and the Pharisees went to Pilate.*

The 24ₜₕ day refer Sunday (The first day of creation)

On the Sunday was the victory of God, it's clear that after this very day, The Lord departed to prepared a place for his Holy people, this 24ᵗʰ Sunday was written by all the prophets pointing this 24ᵗʰ day, like when they saw the vision of a men clothed in linen, the prophets saw the Lord's glory, which was not the temple, was his body like the crown of God Almighty, and the crown is eternal life because he lives forever and ever, he is who spoke about Sunday through the ancient

prophets in the book of Genesis in symbolic days and symbolic personalities, and yes, Sunday refer the beginning of all creation.

Mark 16:9 **When Jesus rose early on the first day of the week, he appeared first to Mary Magdalene,** *out of whom he had driven seven demons.*

John 20:1 **Early on the first day of the week, while it was still dark,** *Mary Magdalene went to the tomb and saw that the stone had been removed from the entrance.*

Sunday was the beginning of all creation because the father did send his sons and daughters as if each one of them were his only one son and loving them as if they were one, but the Lord sent them not to condemned the world but to save the world through them, that whoever believes in them that Jesus is the Lord shall be saved, and so now we increased in number, just as it is written by the ancient prophets in the book of Genesis:

Genesis 1:3 **And God said, "Let there be light," and there was light.**

And by faith we understand that this was fulfilled in the beginning **by the word of God;**

Matthew 4: 14 **"You are the light of the world.** *A town built on a hill*

Can't be hidden. 15 Neither do people light a lamp and put it under a bowl.

Instead they put it on its stand, and it gives light to everyone in the house.

16 In the same way, **let your light shine before others,** *that they may see your good deeds and glorify your Father in heaven.*

But also God saw that the light was good, **that's why Creation will be accomplish with separation** and so until the end of the age this will continually be;

Genesis 1: 4 God saw that the light was good, and he separated the light from the darkness.

In conclusion on this chapter, Sunday is the beginning and discloses Sabbath day-Saturday-as the end of the age and so the end of God's creation as well.

CHAPTER 05

THE GLORY OF GOD

Sunday the 24th Day as symbolism.

In the book of revelation the creation starts with Jesus Christ's victory through suffered death by his own bother(s) this repeats in different points of view also this is the reason why the vision is misunderstood in the prophetic and biblical speech in which our Lord is the author.

To be in the Spirit is to be in the Word of God, this is symbolic and refer to listen with an understanding ear and close attention.

Here are the six days of creation represented as **144,000** as the first foundation is made of jasper refer the Lord's victory that is the first day of creation, and the six foundation called ruby or carnelian refer the six days of creation but the six days of creation are based in only one day which is **"Sunday."**

Revelation 4:[2] *At once I was in the Spirit, and there before me was a throne in heaven with someone sitting on it.* [3] *And the one who sat there had the appearance of **jasper and ruby...***

1ˢᵗ **The first foundation was** jasper_____1__the throne in heaven

2ⁿᵈ the second foundation sapphire_____4

3ʳᵈ the third foundation agate_____4

4ᵗʰ the fourth foundation emerald_____0

5ᵗʰ the fifth foundation onyx_____0

6ᵗʰ **the sixth foundation** ruby or Carnelian____0

The 144,000 is the seal of the living God, its true meaning refer the first day of creation that is "Sunday the 24ᵗʰ day" and the rainbow is like an emerald around the throne, and emerald refer the fourth seal of four numbers known as 1,000 years.

The first day of creation is Sunday the 24ᵗʰ day and its true meaning is hidden by the 1,000 years, and as the 1,000 years refer the first day of creation as Sunday the 24ᵗʰ day, also discloses the last day of creation that is Sabbath day, this day is Saturday also known as 1,000 years as well.

*Revelation 4:³... **A rainbow that shone like an emerald** encircled the throne.*

2 peter 3:⁸ But do not forget this one thing, dear friends: With the Lord **a day is like a thousand years,** and **a thousand years are like a day.**

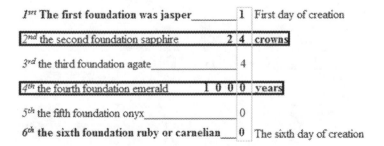

1ˢᵗ **The first foundation was jasper**_____1 │ First day of creation

2ⁿᵈ the second foundation sapphire   2 │ 4 │ crowns

3ʳᵈ the third foundation agate_____4

4ᵗʰ the fourth foundation emerald   1 0 0 0 │ years

5ᵗʰ the fifth foundation onyx_____0

6ᵗʰ **the sixth foundation ruby or carnelian**___0 │ The sixth day of creation

Sunday the 24th day was the day when the Lord's temple was rebuild with a chronologic sign of three days, Sunday was the third day referring Jesus' body being rebuild. In the same way the 24 thrones refer Friday, the 24 Elders refer Saturday, the 24 crowns and the white robes refer the third day that is Sunday also the first day of creation.

*Revelation 4:[4] Surrounding the throne were **twenty-four** other thrones, and seated on them were **twenty-four elders**. They were dressed in white and had **crowns of gold on their heads.***

Sunday the 24th day was the day of the Lord's victory over death, just like the three chronological days as a sign of the temple being rebuild on the third day that is Sunday and the first day of creation. In the same way the four living creatures are four chronological days before the day of the Lord's victory over death, these four days are based from a 21rst day to 24th day; The lion represent the 21rst day referring Thursday, the ox represent the 22nd day referring Friday, the one with a face like a man represent the 23rd day referring Saturday (Sabbath), and finally the eagle represent the 24th day, and the 24 which has two numbers, those two numbers refer the two wings of the great eagle, this discloses the first day of creation that is Sunday and symbolized as the 24.

*Revelation 4:[7] The first living creature was like a lion, the second was like an ox, the third had a face like a man, **the fourth was like a flying eagle.** [8] Each of the four living creatures **had six wings** and was covered with eyes all around, even under its wings…*

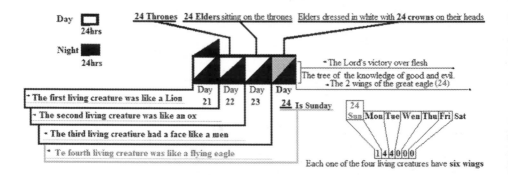

The 24 represent the two wings of the great eagle and Sunday as the first day of creation, and the creation is based in seven days, six days of work and the seventh day is when God rested from all his work of creation, this is figuratively called as done simply because God spoke through the prophets that, what is done must take place before it's fulfilment, otherwise it wouldn't be written with no will.

In God's creation are six days of work and those days are based on **Sunday (the first day of creation)** and so the Great day of the Lord is revealed as **Saturday (Sabbath day) the last day on God's creation.**

In the same way the **144,000** represent the six days of creation which are based in the **24** (Sunday, the first day of creation), and the hour is hidden among the seven eyes, simply because every eye on the seven continents will see the Lord at his coming with thousands upon thousands of his holy ones, even the ones who right now are sleeping on the dust of the ground and this refers the final resurrection. In the seven eyes is hidden the hour of the Lord's appearing on heaven:

20-**0,000,000.**

This is how we know who is our Lord and God, because he didn't came in the world to sit on his throne, he proved that he is worthy of glory and honor and power, he suffered to give us understanding, not sleeping well, nor eating well, always ready to make sure that everything was on its on time and place, while he was here, he protected his followers, healing the hurt, giving comfort to the needy, protecting the repented sinner and forgiving with his compassion, the one that in the Holy Scriptures it is written as creation, for we are created by love, Jesus Christ suffered greatly by the Jewish leaders (his brothers), and then by their guards, then by the unreasoning punishment that Pilate inflict on him, then not enough with it, he was sentenced to be crucified by all the city and no authority intervention, for the governor washed his hands as Jesus was given to put to death, and its written, he was worthy, because he didn't do it to get glory, he did it for our salvation, and so we are his glory as we are his temple, he did it simply, majesty and uniquely for the love that he have for all of us. That's the reason why the first day of creation which was Sunday is to keep in mind like a seal on our foreheads, because on that day the Lord have blessing the humanity.

Revelation 4:[10]*…They lay **their crowns** before **the throne** and say:*

[11] ***"You are worthy, our Lord and God,***
to receive glory and honor and power,
for you created all things,
and by your will they were created
and have their being."

Chapter 06

THE SCROLL WITH 7 SEALS

The book of Revelation is the scroll writing on both sides, because on one side it has seven eyes and on the other side it has seven signs, just like in one side it has seven trumpets of God Almighty and on the other side it has seven bowls of wrath of God Almighty. Also on the book of revelation there are seven seals where the hour and day of God's coming is hidden, to read and to understand clearly the Holy Scriptures is needed to understand how the seven seals are open and then the conclusion of all things is revealed, for its meant to be revealed because the time of its fulfilment is near at the door.

*Revelation 5:1 Then I saw in the right hand of him who sat on the throne a scroll with writing on both sides and **sealed with seven seals.***

The sixth seal represent the six days of creation starting with Sunday **(144,000)** Sunday is revealed as **24**, it is very important to keep in mind that Sunday is the first day of creation. On the seventh day God rested from all the work of creating that he had done, is revealed as Saturday known as Sabbath but since the day is disclosed on the seventh day, the hour is hidden in the seventh seal represented with seven zeroes (20)**0,000,000** Only our heavenly father knows the day and the hour of the end, he disclosed it in signs, he send angels to guide, to prepared the flock of the great shepherd, we as instruments for his creation are to sing this song, that he was worthy in the beginning, and will be worthy at the end for ever and ever, amen!

Here are the six days of creation **(144,000)**, all of this refer symbolically the Sunday **(24)**.

One number refer the first seal--------------------*1*

Two numbers refer the second seal--------------*24*----= 12 + 12.

Three numbers refer third seal-----------------*144*----= 12 x 12.

Four numbers refer the fourth seal----------*1,000*

Five numbers refer the fifth seal------------*12,000*----= 12 x 1,000.

Six numbers refer the sixth seal-----------*144,000*----= 12 x 12,000.

Since the seventh day of creation is the end known as Sabbath (Saturday) in the seventh seal it's found the hour is hidden as the seven eyes that will see God's coming at the appointed time of the end because all eye will see him (**20**:00hrs)

Seven numbers refer the seventh seal-----------*20-0,000,000*

In the book of Revelation chapter five, Michael is represented as the angel who makes questions knowing the answers, one of the elders refer the 24, which means Sunday the 24th day and also the first day of creation when the root of David triumphed.

And when it says the Lion of the tribe of Judah refer the first living creature which was place in the 21rst day **on Thursday, when Jesus Christ have dinner with his twelve disciples,** *the day of Unleavened Bread on which the Passover Lamb had to be sacrificed.*

Revelation 5: [5] *Then one of the elders said to me,* **"Do not weep! See, the Lion of the tribe of Judah, the Root of David, has triumphed. He is able to open the scroll and its seven seals."** [6] *Then I saw a Lamb, looking as if it had been slain, standing at the center of the throne, encircled by the four living creatures and the elders. The Lamb had seven horns and seven eyes, which are the seven spirits of God sent out into all the earth.*

Jesus' victory on Sunday (the first day of creation) repeats constantly in the Holy Scriptures even in the book of Revelation as well, this is the reason is misunderstood the creation. We, represent the Lamb, as the Lion triumphed we must triumph in order to save our friends, that is our holy family, preparing them for the coming salvation and from the coming wrath of God almighty, when we have a clear and simple understanding of the new name of our Lord and God, and that he is our heavenly father, uniquely because he was worthy, his victory is like a new love song that we must keep in mind just as his name, "**Jesus Christ**".

Revelation 5:[9] ***And they sang a new song, saying:***

"You are worthy …

Chapter 07

"THE FIRST DAY OF CREATION"

THE FIRST SEAL

The first seal is based in the understanding of God's throne as "1" The first seal refer the first day of creation, but is a sequence of four seals to understand the meaning of the four days of creation as well. Here is the first seal but only counts when the fourth seal is revealed:

Revelation 6:[1] *I watched as the Lamb opened the first of the seven seals.*

```
0-0-0-4-4-1    <=== Sunday
0--------2-4
0-------1-4-4
4----1-0-0-0
4-1-2-0-0-0
1-4-4-0-0-0
```

The 21rst day refer Thursday (The Lamb of God). On Thursday was the last supper, when Jesus Christ have dinner with his twelve apostles, *the day of Unleavened Bread on which the Passover Lamb had to be sacrificed. It was the day when Judas Iscariot betrayed him, and its clear how Thursday is symbolically called the 21rst day which refer the first living creature "the lion":*

Revelation 6:[1] *Then I heard one of the four living creatures say in a voice like thunder, "Come!"*

The Lion refer the Lord's victory apart of the chronological sequence of the four living creatures. Its true representation is the first day of creation, don't be surprised if you see Sunday the 24th day repeatable in symbolism, because it's the climax of the six days and the four days of creation. Here is the sign of the beginning and also the Lord's victory over flesh, symbolically called the rider is Jesus Christ and the white horse is Judea as it is written in the book of the prophet Zacharias chapter ten verse three,"

...the LORD *Almighty will care for his flock, the people of Judah, and make them like a proud horse in battle."*

The white throne, the white horse and the white clothes refer the righteous acts of the saints, God's Holy people.

This refer Thursday, the 21[rst] day, and the first living creature on symbolic speech.

Revelation 6:[2] I looked, and there before me was a white horse! Its rider held a bow, and he was given a crown, and he rode out as a conqueror bent on conquest.

THE SECOND SEAL

The second seal is based in two numbers like "12+12=**24**" The second seal is part of the four seals like the sequence of the four days of creation, this refer the separation of the heavens from the earth, and its final solution is the first day of creation (Sunday), but the four seals counts only when the fourth seal is revealed, here is the second seal:

Revelation 6:[3] When the Lamb opened the second seal...

```
0-0-0-4-4-1
0------ -2-4  ⇦  12x12=24
0-----1-4-4
4---1-0-0-0
4-1-2-0-0-0
1-4-4-0-0-0
```

The 22nd day refer Friday. On Friday, Jesus was crucified by his brothers (spiritual speech) Jesus was meant to overcome before he was born. For now this is Friday, the 22nd day, when his blood cleans us from our sins, that's how we became his Sons and daughters, there's no greater love than this, inexplicable because it was the creator's desired to be sacrifice for our salvation, his blood was forgiveness of our sins, because his sufferings were exceeding great, this refer Friday, the 22nd day, and the second living creature on symbolic speech.

Revelation 6:^{3} *…I heard the second living creature say, "Come!"*

Michael is the Lord's helper, this occurs in the last days, just as it is writing in the book of Revelation, chapter twelve, verse seven;

"Then war broke out in heaven. Michael and his angels fought against the dragon, and the dragon and his angels fought back."

This is the correct representation for the red dragon "The accuser", Michael and his angels overcame the dragon and his angels by the blood of the Lamb, this means that this take place after our Lord's victory, he gave us victory over that ancient serpent called the devil, or Satan, who leads the whole world astray.

Revelation 6:^{4} *Then another horse came out, a fiery red one. Its rider was given power to take peace from the earth and to make people kill each other. To him was given a large sword.*

THE THIRD SEAL

The third seal is part of the fourth seal based in three numbers "12x12=**144**" but its true interpretation is part of the four days of creation, but the four seals are only count when the fourth seal is revealed, here is the third seal and its interpretation:

Revelation 6:^{5} *When the Lamb opened the third seal,*

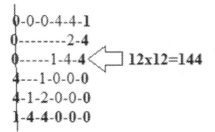

The 23rd day refer the Saturday. On Sabbath day, the Pharisees asked Pilate to make secured the tomb were Jesus body was lying down, and Pilate agreed to do as they asked him, he ordered to take guards with them to make secured the tomb were Jesus Christ was buried so no one could open the grave were Jesus body was lying down. And so they did it. In the Holy Scriptures doesn't say much about this particular day, just that it was Sabbath, the 23rd day, also the third living creature on symbolic speech except the Jewish feast on Sabbath.

*Revelation 6:*⁵ *...I heard the third living creature say, "Come!"*

The first beast refers the government of a continent (Kingdom) a union of ten nations (10 horns) ten nations also refer waters which are peoples, multitudes, nations and languages. The union of ten nations will be different from all the other continents (kingdoms) and will devour the whole earth, trampling it down and crushing it. This is the meaning of a great war and will affect the supplies of food worldwide, but it won't last long, only until the time of wrath of God Almighty is completed for it must take place and will last shortly.

*Revelation 6:*¹ *I looked, and there before me was a black horse!* **Its rider was holding a pair of scales in his hand.**

THE FOURTH SEAL

The fourth seal is based in four numbers "**1-0-0-0**" this is the end of the sequence of the four seals "**1,000 years**". Also the end of the sequence of the four living creatures from Thursday, the 21st day to Sunday **the 24th**

day, day of our Lord's victory. And the understanding of the first four days of separation in creation as well on symbolic speech.

All of these means that the fourth seal is **(1,000 years)** and the fourth of the living creatures is the symbolic representation for the day of Sunday **(24)** just as it is written: "for our Lord a thousand years are like a day and a day is like a thousand years".

Now is simple to understand: the fourth seal (1-0-0-0) is like the first day of creation (Sunday), and the last day of creation is like the four seal as well" because when the thousand seal is open, it reveals the first day of creation that was hidden on it, and as soon as the Sunday is revealed as the first day of creation and the first day of the week, we logically understand that the end of the week and the seventh day is Saturday, in this way the last day of creation of God's coming is revealed, something that was hidden with the fourth seal (1,000 years), This is our true testimony that must be finish before the end of the age, now you understand that its fulfilment is near.

Revelation 6:[7] *When the Lamb opened the fourth seal…*

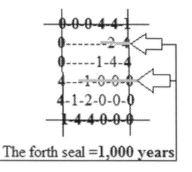

The forth seal =1,000 years

The 24th **day refer Sunday (The first day of creation). On the Sunday was the victory of God, it's clear that after this very day, The Lord departed to prepared a place for his Holy people, this 24**th **Sunday was written by all the prophets pointing this 24**th **day, when they saw the visions and saw the Lord's glory, which was not the temple, was his body like the crown of God Almighty, and the crown is eternal life because he lives forever and ever, he is who spoke about Sunday through the ancient prophets in the book of Genesis in**

symbolic days and in symbolic personalities, and yes, Sunday refer the beginning of all creation. This very day is Sunday, the 24th day, and the fourth living creature, the great eagle's wings simply because is based on two numbers (24) this is a day to give to the church (the bride) so they may understand that we have to be prepared in baptism and spirit because its fulfilment is near, Amen.

Revelation 6:[7] ...I heard the voice of the fourth living creature say, "Come!"

The last enemy of God is figuratively called "death" on the first day of creation the physical action and reaction (death) was defeated when Jesus Christ raise from the grave, the first day of creation. But in the last days it appoints a future governor "death" which is the rider of the pale horse, the pale horse refer peoples, multitudes, nations and languages, also called hades, and the pale horse (hades) follows death. Three days and a half are appointed and the mark of the beast brakes the sixth commandment those three days just like it is written in the Holy Scriptures:

Exodus 20:[13] "You shall not murder.

But at the end of those three days with their nights, death will exist no more, but I will encourage you to keep this in mind for it concerns the salvation of humanity, "Do not murder" it's true that there is forgiveness of all sins but if you kill by the sword understand that you shall be killed by sword, and pray so that you may find favor with the Lord at the day of judgment.

Do not be deceived, for the seal of the living God is part of a chronological sequence of seven seals, the seals doesn't have nothing in common with the mark of the beast, people will be forced to take it or be put to death, but the seven open seals are an understanding of the Holy scriptures and the Holy Scriptures are God's words.

Revelation 6:[8] I looked, and there before me was a pale horse! Its rider was named Death, and Hades was following close behind him. They were given power over a fourth of the earth to kill by sword, famine and plague, and by the wild beasts of the earth.

Chapter 08

THE HARVEST OF THE EARTH

THE FIFTH SEAL

The four horns and the golden altar that is before God

In the fifth seal there is a new representation of the appointed time of God's coming.

The four angels are a tetrad of four moons when they turned blood red, the four horns of the golden altar are the four winds of the earth and in the fifth seal is represented the earth as the golden altar.

In the four angels is found the month and year because the chronological sequence of the moon's phases is based in thirty days each new moon and the new year as well, because the year is based on the moon's cycle around the earth even if the present calendar is not based on the exact moon's cycle worldwide. This is God's work biblically and prophetically, it is important to count the moon to show the seasons and even to rip the harvest of what is sow.

Revelation 6:⁹ When he opened the fifth seal...

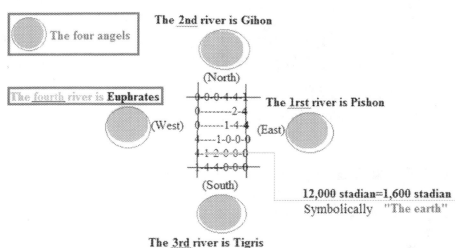

On the fifth seal the earth is represented as the golden altar the golden altar is based on the earth and the souls of those who had been killed because of the word of God and the testimony they maintained remained under the altar, or under the earth, they are physically sleeping on the dust of the ground while the soul (as believers) awaits for the Great day of the Lord, and the crown of life for eternal peace, this will take place at the very end of the age, for it is written in the book of Hebrews chapter eleven verses: thirty-eight, thirty-nine and forty;

"the world was not worthy of them. They wandered in deserts and mountains, living in caves and in holes in the ground. These were all commended for their faith, **yet none of them received what had been promised, since God had planned something better for us so that only together with us would they be made perfect".**

But we are on the fifth seal were the month and year is disclosed, ones God discloses for his holy people the appointed time of the end, we are just servants in order to serve the preparation for the new age that is coming to be eternal, like a gift from God's hand that we must be worthy to receive from him who loved us before everything was created, we were created for him and by him, Amen.

*Revelation 6:⁹ ...I saw **under the altar the souls** of those who had been slain because of the word of God and the testimony they had maintained.*

"LAST DAY OF CREATION"
THE SIXTH SEAL

The seal of the living God that is symbolically based in six numbers "1-4-4-0-0-0" as a seal refers the six days of God's work on the creation of the world.

The first day of creation is Sunday, and the fourth day in a the sequence of the four living creatures is the 24. Also referring Sunday as the 24th day the four living creatures also represent a thousand years as a seal of four numbers (1-0-0-0) that's the reason why, for the Lord, a day is like a thousand years. As we can see, the Holy Scriptures written in prophecy and symbolism is not writing to read literally, the creation of mankind is written with seven seals, ones God opens them these reveals God's plan (he does open the seals through his servants), but it's important because it reveals the appointed time of the beginning and the most important now is the appointed time of the end, this is to be prepared.

In the same way the sixth seal is base in six numbers "1-4-4-0-0-0" represent the first day of creation "24" that is Sunday, so for the 144,000 its final solution is the first day of creation "Sunday" the day of Jesus Christ's victory over flesh.

The 144,000 it's the number of the Servants of our God, but is not the counting of how many they are, having understood Sunday as the 24th day, the 144,000 seal becomes the seal that discloses who is our heavenly father and the creator of all the living.

Here is the sixth seal opened, just like the six days of creation refer the first day of creation, so the sixth seal refer Sunday like the 24th day and logically discloses the last day of creation as well like "**Sunday 24 and Saturday 24**", just like it's written in the second book of peter chapter three verse eight;

*"But do not forget this one thing, dear friends: With the Lord **a day is like a thousand years**, and **a thousand years are like a day**".*

Revelation 6:[12] I watched as he opened the sixth seal...

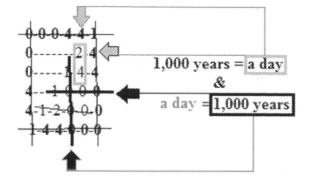

At the end of the age on the last day of creation God revealed that will occurred a great earthquake, but we are on the sixth seal which represent the first and the last day of creation as "24" which is the 144,000 seal that covered the day of judgment from the eyes of unbelievers of Jesus Christ.

Revelation 6:[12] ...There was a great earthquake...

After the sign of the day, here repeats the complementation of the month and year, we know this because the moon gives the signs of the year together with the sun in a cycle of thirty days, now we know the sign of the son of men that is written in the book of Matthew, chapter twenty-four, verses twenty-nine and thirty:

"the sun will be darkened, and the moon will not give its light; *...* *"Then will appear the sign of the Son of Man in heaven. And then all the peoples of the earth will mourn when they see the Son of Man coming on the clouds of heaven, with power and great glory."*

The sun darkened and the moon not giving its light refer an eclipsed, then it's written the sign of the son of Man which in other chapters we logically can understand that is the sign of the moon when it turned blood red, these are the signs in heaven above and they refer God's coming.

Here is another chapter that explains in a logical writing in the Holy Scriptures, the sign of the son of Man in a different point of view in the book of the prophet Joel, chapter two, verses thirty and thirty one;

*I will show wonders **in the heavens** and on the earth, blood and fire and billows of smoke. **The sun will be turned to darkness** and the moon to blood before the coming of the great and dreadful day of the* LORD.

The signs in the heavens below are referring a great war, that's why war is explained on the earth as blood and fire and billows of smoke. Now here are the signs on the heavens above, it repeats that the sun will be turned to darkness and also repeats that the moon to blood, but it is logically the sign of the month explained before the great and dreadful day of the Lord. Ones more, here is the eclipsed and the moon turned to blood and those are signs on the heavens above, this also is repeated on the book of Acts spoke by the apostle Peter to the Jews who live in Jerusalem the day of Pentecost. After Peter spoke the signs in the heavens above and the earth below, Peter addressed the day of the Lord like a great and glorious day.

When God opens the sixth seal through his servants, it's revealed the signs of his coming, in the book of John "Revelation" the wonders in the heavens above refer the sun turned to black and the moon turned to blood red, then stars falling to the earth as a literally speech because the clearance of the objects that he speaks about. On the next written verses, explains how the four winds of the earth are lost after the signs of heaven above with the sun and the moon and the stars.

Revelation 6:[12] *...**The sun turned black like sackcloth made of goat hair,** the whole moon turned blood red,* [13] *and the stars in the sky fell to earth, as figs drop from a fig tree when shaken by a strong wind.* [14] *The heavens receded like a scroll being rolled up, and every mountain and island was removed from its place.*

The four angels represent a moon cycle when it turns blood red, called"the tetrad" because the moon turning blood red is based on a cycle of four moons, this is a sign for all the nations and the good news of the seven thunders which message is faster, like lightning and thundering over the earth, for it addresses the signs of the Lord's coming.

Just as the four rivers written in the book of Genesis are called: Pishon, Gihon, Tigris and the fourth is the river Euphrates, so that's how the sign of the son of men will be, with the fourth moon turned blood red.

This is why the four angels are bound at the great river Euphrates, because the tetrad of the moon turned blood red refer the four angels, and the four horns of the golden altar are the four winds of the earth, and the golden altar is referring the earth as well.

Ones the fourth moon appears in heaven, by then, it is the sign of the son of Man, and there shall be just a matter of days before the great day of the Lord to be fulfilled all prophesy.

- When God appears in heaven in fulfilment of the vision then each one of you will acknowledge our Heavenly Father, because the son will sit at his right side and you daughters and sons of God represent the son of God, Amen!

*Revelation 7:[1] After this **I saw four angels standing at the four corners of the earth,** holding back the four winds of the earth to prevent any wind from blowing on the land or on the sea or on any tree. [2] Then I saw another angel coming up from the east, having the seal of the living God. He called out in a loud voice to **the four angels** who had been given power to harm the land and the sea: [3] "Do not harm the land or the sea or the trees until we put a seal on the foreheads of the servants of our God." [4] Then I heard the number of those who were sealed: 144,000 from all the tribes of Israel.*

After the seal of the living God gets understood as the first day of creation, explains the beginning of creation about the Lamb, then it disclosed the end of creation "Saturday" when the Lord comes to take us with him on the clothes of heaven, because Jesus is our Lord of lords.

At God's coming the great multitude that no one could count is found to be dressed in white clothes, standing before the throne of God which is the sky, and standing before the Lamb who is God, this refer the last day of creation as well, and do not be surprised if Sunday and Sabbath repeats figuratively. Remember, this understanding take us to a clear consciousness to acknowledge our father in heaven, knowing this true is like a new song of thanksgiving to our only savior and God.

Revelation 7: [9] *After this I looked, and there before me was **a great multitude that no one could count,** from every nation, tribe, people and language, standing before the throne and before the Lamb. They were wearing white robes and were holding palm branches in their hands.*

"THE LAST HOUR"
THE SEVEN SEAL

The sixth seal "144,000" represent the first day of creation "24" and because in the seventh day of creation is disclosed as the great day of the Lord "Saturday". And because the day is already given in the seventh day of creation, God gave on the seventh seal the appointed hour of his coming like a theft at night. Ones taking out the seventh seal, the hour is disclosed.

And a half an hour it's disclosed as well on the same hour when the great earthquake is revealed after God's coming and all eye will see him, that's why the seventh seal refer also the seven eyes which is the appointed time of the end.

The seventh seal is based in seven numbers "20 [**0-0-0-0-0-0-0**]" ones taking out the seventh seals our Lord and Father revealed us the hour of his coming.

Here on the seven seals it's found the hour, the day, the month and the year. We, as his servants, are instruments to prepare our Holy family with God's advice.

Revelation 8: [1] *When he opened the seventh seal…*

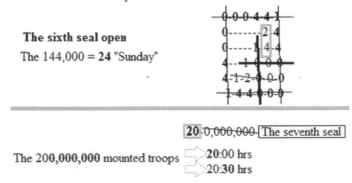

The sixth seal open
The 144,000 = 24 "Sunday"

20-0,000,000 [The seventh seal]

The 200,000,000 mounted troops · 20:00 hrs
20:30 hrs

Revelation 8:[1] *...there was silence in heaven for about* **half an hour.**

After the seventh seal there are seven trumpets, to be sound by the seven angels, the seven angels represent the two witnesses because they stand before the Lord of the earth, this is a prophesy to be fulfilled at the last day of creation, the two witnesses will stand in the presence of the Lord at his coming, also known as the two fiery pillars.

But first the trumpets are sounding like seven warnings to the inhabitants of the earth, and preparation for the Holy City to be dressed in white clothing by baptism.

Revelation 8:[2] *And I saw the seven angels who stand before God, and seven trumpets were given to them.*

Chapter 09

TEN DAYS

THE 1ᴿˢᵀ WOE!-TEN DAYS

The seven trumpets have no chronologic sequence. The seven trumpets are in an order of four phases, the first one is called **"The first woe!"** The second one is called **"The second woe!"** The third one is called **"The third woe!"** And the fourth one is called **"A third"** keeping in mind this order, you will understand the seven trumpets, the seven seals holds the appointed time of the end, but the seven trumpets, gives the last ten days with its the three days and a half, and also the place where this will come to be fulfilled before its end.

The fifth angel is the first call or the first woe! It's represented as the great eagle with **two wings** and the two **wings** refer the first Day of creation as Sunday the **24**ᵗʰ, the flying eagle is in representation the message of God, even the servants of God.

Revelation 8:[13] *...* ***"Woe! Woe! Woe*** *to the inhabitants of the earth, because of the trumpet blasts about to be sounded by the other* ***three angels!"***

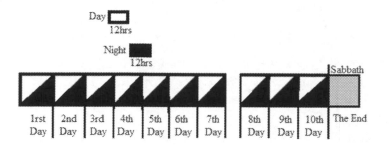

In the first trumpet it's found a great war that broke out on the earth by the falling of one star, and this star on the fifth trumpet refer Satan, and in the book of the apostle Luke chapter ten verse eighteen is written how our Lord saw Satan fall like lightning from heaven, this is literal speech but… our Lord Jesus saw Satan falling from heaven and as a prophetic speech is the end of the war in heaven when Michael and his angels fought against Satan and his angels, and Satan and his angels fought back, but Satan and his angels lost their place in heaven, Michael and his angels overcame him by the blood of the Lamb, which means that this refer a prophesy of the last days before the conclusion of creation, but literally our Lord Jesus Christ refer this verse of the star falling from heaven that is repeat in the book of Revelation with a prophetic speech in symbolism, the sky is heaven, and heaven is on the earth as well, before the Holy City leaves where it belongs, the sky. But Satan is even in heaven before the end comes, and so the end of Satan will come:

Luke 10: [18] *He replied, "**I saw Satan fall like lightning from heaven.***

Revelation 9:[1] *The fifth angel sounded his trumpet, and I saw a **star that had fallen from the sky to the earth.** The star was given the key to the shaft of the Abyss.*

And when he opens the abyss which is literally called, "Abyss" for there is no other representation for it, except that divides humanity, the heaven from the hell. Then after the abyss, the destructor makes his appearing, first in the city of Jerusalem, this prophetic speech is based on 10 days before the end, 10 days are symbolically represented by five months also one hundred fifty days, 10 days are the set times.

*Revelation 9: [5] They were not allowed to kill them but only to torture them for **five months.***

*Revelation 9:[10] They had tails with stingers, like scorpions, and in their tails they had power to torment people for **five months.***

In the book of Genesis this great war of 10 days over the surface of the earth is symbolically represented as the great flood of one hundred fifty days, the one hundred fifty days are written this way to hide the appointed time of the end, the great flood is an important part in a prophetic speech of the 10 days of great war, and here are the days:

*Genesis 7: [24] The waters flooded the earth for a **150 days.***

*Genesis 8:[3] The water receded steadily from the earth, at the end of the **150 days** the water had gone down.*

In the book of Daniel, the vision concerning the daily sacrifice, the rebellion that causes desolation, the surrender of the sanctuary and the trampling underfoot of the LORD's people will last 10 days. The great war of 10 days over the surface of the earth was given to understand in the book of Daniel, it is written as 2,300 days and nights, but in full days without divide them by days with its nights are 1,150 full days, now the number two on the 2,300 refer days and nights, and the number one on the 1,150 refer a full day, in based of the signs of the 2=days and nights, and 1=full days, there is only left 150 days, this days are symbolic and refer the 10 days of the great war over the surface of the earth..

*Daniel 8: [14] He said to me, "It will take **2,300 evenings and mornings;** then the sanctuary will be reconsecrated."*

In the book of revelation the 150 days of the great flood and the 2,300 days and nights are clear by God's words in the book of Revelation and this concludes the entire scriptures concerning the 10 days of war before end of the age. Here it's clear how our Lord and God give us comfort with his own words and with no seals here, he explained with a clear speech that there will be 10 days of a great persecution over the surface of the earth, this is the reason why the seven letters are sent to the seven churches referring all the churches on the seven continents of the earth, each letter for a single continent. But we are here on the fifth trumpet which is the first woe!

It's also clear by God's words that after those 10 days he will come to give us the crown of life which is the eternal life, this is not a simple gift, but only God can give it, even the white robes that we will be dressing on.

Revelation 2:[10] *Do not be afraid of what you are about to suffer. I tell you, the devil will put some of you in prison to test you, and you will suffer persecution for* **ten days**. *Be faithful, even to the point of death, and I will give you life as your victor's crown.*

In the book of Jeremiah it's clear how the prophet by the Spirit of God prophesied about the last 10 days and this repeats in all the books of the Prophets of God, and explains that by those 10 days of great war the people that doesn't live in Jerusalem shall returned to their own lands, because of the terrible disaster that looms out of the north, this is to be prepared, and this is for the safety of God's Holy people, as soon as you get the understanding you shall not be on those days of wrath over the dessert between the seas and the beautiful holy mountain, as it is written in the book of Daniel chapter eleven verse forty-five:

He will pitch his royal tents between the seas at the beautiful holy mountain…

In the holy scriptures all that is written will be fulfilled, but this is before the end of the age, and points Jerusalem as the center of the great war, and persecution over the surface of the earth, this refer something out of control, and as Jeremiah explained in his book by the spirit of God.

Jeremiah 6:1"Flee for safety, people of Benjamin! **Flee from Jerusalem!** *Sound the trumpet in Tekoa! Raise the signal over Beth Hakkerem!* <u>For disaster looms out of the north, even terrible destruction.</u>

In the book of the prophet Zechariah refer Jerusalem as part of the land of the north, its understandable because this is the spiritual speech to call us out of the Land of the north for safety, this repeats and there is only 10 days of persecution and prison and even death, God gave us announcements about those 10 days but at the end, there shall be no more death, no more pain, no more hunger and no more thirst.

Zechariah 2:[6] *"Come! Come! Flee from the <u>land of the north,</u>" declares the Lord,*

This is a message to proclaimed with joy, because there is an appointed time for all this trouble to come to its end, and all of this is for the deliverance of all the ones who are written in the book of life, the book of the Lamb, even just anyone who call in the name of the lord at that day, he or she shall be saved. So this is to proclaim with shouts of join, to leave from the destruction of Babylon like Lot left Sodom, and like Israel left Egypt, but its true meaning is the final resurrection on the last day of creation.

Isaiah 48: [20] <u>*Leave Babylon, flee from the Babylonians!*</u> *Announce this with shouts of joy and proclaim it. <u>Send it out to the ends of the earth</u>;*

Now in the book of the prophet Jeremiah its symbolically explained how the people of God who lives in the city of Babylon shall say to each other as a prophesy to be occurred before the 10 days begins and lapsed over Babylon (figurative speech).

Jeremiah 51: [9] *"'We would have healed Babylon, but she cannot be healed; <u>let us leave her and each go to our own land,</u> for her judgment reaches to the skies, it rises as high as the heavens.'*

In the book of the prophet Jeremiah its symbolically explain how the enemies of Jerusalem will talk about the attack against her, in a prophetic speech it is disclosed.

Jeremiah 6:[4] *"Prepare for battle against her! Arise, <u>let us attack at noon!</u> But, alas, the day light is fading, and the shadows of evening grow long.*[5] *So arise, <u>let us attack at night and destroy her fortresses!</u>"*

In the book of Luke, one of the twelve disciples of Jesus Christ our Lord, he spoke about Jesus' words when he approach to Jerusalem, and on chapter nineteen it says that when Jesus saw the city of Jerusalem, he wept over her, and say this:

Luke 19: [41] *As he approached Jerusalem and saw the city, he wept over it* [43] *The days will come upon you when your enemies will build an embankment against you and encircle you and hem you in on every side.* [44] *They will dash you to the ground, you and the children within your walls. They will not leave one stone on another, because you did not recognize the time of God's coming to you."*

Jesus Christ prophesied in this chapter with his great authority that the city of Jerusalem will be destroyed and her walls completely tear down, and in the book of Matthew chapter twenty-four verse one and two, also explains the total destruction of the temple of Jerusalem, and this will be an abomination that causes desolation. This is why you must be prepared because those 10 days means great war, but you shall stand, because at the end of those 10 days the Lord shall give us the crown of life.

Matthew 24: [1, 2] *Jesus left the temple and was walking away when his disciples came up to him to call his attention to its buildings. "Do you see all these things?" he asked. "Truly I tell you, not one stone here will be left on another; everyone will be thrown down."*

CHAPTER 10

THE 2ND WOE!-THREE DAYS AND ONE NIGHT

The seven trumpets doesn't have an order in a chronological sequence, but the order is separated in four phases, the second one is called **"The second woe!"** keeping in mind the true order, is clear to understand the sequence of the seven trumpets, the second woe is also the fifth trumpet.

The fifth trumpet refer three days and a half, but in the book of revelation have three representations; the first representation refer when Elijah prophesied to the Israelites the three years and a half of no rain over the land of Israel and in that way he defeated the four hundred Baal's prophets, by calling on the name of the Lord and the Lord sent rain over the land.

The second representation is when Joseph was advised in a dream to leave from Belem, and take Mary and her child and leave to Egypt, because Herod was searching for the child to kill him, and they stayed in Egypt for a period of three years and a half.

The last representation is the last three days and a half before the end of the God's coming, the three days and a half are also 42 months and also 1,260 days, but the days were shortened because the Lord appointed the three years and a half as three days and a half, and its revealed as three days and one night, because the days are based of twelve hours of day light and twelve hours of night time.

Revelation 9: [12] *The first woe is past;* ***two other woes*** *are yet to come.*

The sixth angel with the sixth trumpet to be sound, refer the angel of the Lord, the one that released the four angels that are bound at the great river Euphrates, this concerns the sign of the moon turned blood red, and this happens when the four angels (a tetrad when the moon turned blood red) were released just like the great river Euphrates is the last one, the appointed time of the end its also revealed and the four angels are released because they were kept ready for this very hour and day, month and year. The fulfilment of this prophesy it's called **"A third".** The four horns of the golden altar refer the four winds of the earth and the Golden altar refer the earth. The judgment over the earth is because of the blood of Abel and as a good seed we are (figuratively called Abel) the sons and daughters of God.

When it says **"a third"** refer the last of the four phases based on the three woes, the wrath of the Lamb, and refers total destruction but as a judgment over the earth.

*Revelation 9:[15] And the four angels who had been kept ready for this very hour and day and month and year were released to kill **a third of mankind.***

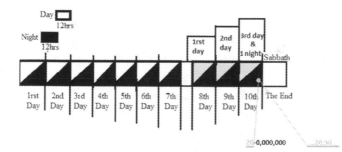

The vision of the other angel with the little scroll refer Jesus' coming, as a vision it has several meanings on each one of its aspects.

When our Lord appears in the sky and with the clouds of heaven is an event that concerns creation and this is the meaning of the head of the angel. And the rainbow above his head refer the Lord's glory, his face was like the sun and as the appearing of the sun in creation occurs the separation of the light from darkness, light means life, seems to be the final resurrection.

The legs of the angel in this vision, represent the servants of God and all who is victorious in his name, when the Lord appears in the sky is also a symbolic speech, the Lord is the temple and the door open in heaven is of the temple's door to enter to the paradise of God which is the sky, for he say in the book of Revelation chapter three verse twelve:

"The one who is victorious I will make a pillar in the temple of my God."

In the seven letters the Lord refer himself as a second or third person, for he say in the book of Revelation chapter two verse twenty-eight; *"I will also give that one the morning star"* but we know that he is the morning star as he says in the book of Revelation chapter twenty-two verse sixteen: *"I am the Root and the Offspring of David, and the bright Morning Star."* this refer God's coming. And we know who will give us the crown of life as well, this is referred in the book of Revelation chapter two verse ten; *"…and I will give you life as your victor's crown."*

At God's coming the final resurrection will occurred, and the death in Jesus will stand from the dust, this refer the fulfilment of creation written in the book of Genesis, as we know. And as the death in Christ rise first, they will be like two fiery pillars, the fire means judgment over the inhabitants of the earth at the fulfilment of all prophesy, for they will see the pillars of God-those who sustains the temple in heaven at God's appearing in the sky-it will burned them as judgment over the unbeliever heart.

Remember that the vision of the other angel, and the representation of the vision refer God's coming on the clouds of heaven, the angel and the servants are angels of the Lord, the ones who have the seal of the living God which was give it to them by God himself through the Holy Scriptures. This shall be fulfilled before the end of the age.

Revelation 10:[1] *Then I saw another mighty angel coming down from heaven.* [2] *He was robed in a cloud, with a rainbow above his head; his face was like the sun, and* **his legs were like fiery pillars.** *He planted his right foot on the sea and his left foot on the land,*

This is why the angel is standing on the sea and on the land, because he is the one who called out in a loud voice (figuratively) saying to the four angels to wait and do not hurt the land and the sea until the seal of the living God is given to the servants of the Lord and so be sealed with the seal of the living God before his coming, this is to be prepared and concerns protection and salvation.

The little scroll is also called the little book and is important on the last message of God to humanity, it is the testimony of the fulfilment of all prophesy and refer God's coming with an open seal. And the Lord gave the testimony to his angel to give it like a little book that laid open in his hand, and also commands his servants to take the little book from the angel's hand.

*Revelation 10:*² **He was holding a little scroll, which lay open in his hand**...

The voice commands the sixth angel with the sixth trumpet to release the four angels (a tetrad when the moon turned blood red) the four angels were bound at the great river Euphrates (The last of the four rivers) and this sign refer a new year by the sun and a new month only based by the phases of the moon. The voice that commands the sixth angel with the sixth trumpet to sound it, is God's voice through the Holy Scriptures, the way is revealed from God through the Holy Scriptures for the appointed time was sealed to be revealed before its fulfilment.

Then God's voice commands his servants to take the little scroll that laid open in the hand of the other mighty angel that came out of heaven and so the vision will be fulfilled when the servants of God will take and eat the little book from the angel's hand.

*Revelation 10:*⁸ *Then the voice that I had heard from heaven spoke to me once more:* **"Go, take the scroll that lies open in the hand of the angel** *who is standing on the sea and on the land."*

The little scroll is represented like a live coal from the seraphim's hand, the seraphim took the coal from the golden altar which refer the earth, and is the testimony of the appointed time of the end, this repeats several times. In the Book of Isaiah chapter six verse six it's written:

"Then one of the seraphim flew to me **with a live coal in his hand** [7] *With it he touched my mouth and said,* "*See, this has touched your lips; your guilt is taken away and your sin atoned for.*"

When the live coal touched the servant's lips was referring that the servant's guilt is taken away and their sins atoned for. The Little scroll that laid open in the angel's hand, is also written in the book of Ezekiel chapter two verse nine and ten:

"… I saw **a hand stretched out to me. In it was a scroll,** *which he unrolled before me…"*

In the book of Ezekiel, in the book of Isaiah and in the book of Revelation refer the little scroll to be eaten by the Lord's servants, means that God's words must live in our lips and our hearts to be our delight, for the time will come to be prepared, and he is guiding all his holy people by his words and his words are his spirit and his life, because his word and his spirit lives in his holy people, means that we bear his name and so we will live by him and for him.

Jeremiah 15: [16] **When your words came, I ate them; they were my joy and my heart's delight, for I bear your name,** LORD **God Almighty.**

Then after the servants hear the words of the scroll and also see the open seals with its trumpets on their right place, then the servants of God are commanded to prophesy as it is written in the book of Acts chapter two verse seventeen:

"'In the last days, God says,
I will pour out my Spirit on all people.
Your sons and daughters **will prophesy,**
your young men **will see visions,**
your old men **will dream dreams.**

In the book of revelation it's clear the commandment for the servants of the Lord to prophesy about the things to come written in the little scroll that is open, after taking the little book and eat from it the words of the Lord the last command is heard:

Revelation 10:[11] *Then I was told,* **"You must prophesy again** *about many peoples, nations, languages and kings."*

Then the two witnesses refer the two wings of the great eagle as 24 in symbolism is the testimony of Jesus Christ victory in the first day of creation, also the two witnesses refer the two fiery pillars that will stand at the presence of the Lord of the earth "The creator of all the earth", so finally, the two witnesses refer the seven angels standing before God, the ones that were given seven trumpets to be sound.

The two witnesses will prophesy for three days and a half, those days were sealed and are represented as three and a half years, also 42 months, or 1,260 days. With an open seal the three days and a half are revealed as three days and one night. The ten days of the great war will end with the three days and one night as well. But before its fulfilment the days will be revealed.

Revelation 10:[3] *And I will appoint my two witnesses, and they will prophesy for* **1,260 days**, *clothed in sackcloth."*

At the end of their testimony, the two witnesses will be put to death, as the sign of the four angels that are bound at the great river Euphrates which is the fourth one of the four rivers. On those 10 days the beast that comes out of the abyss will attack them, and overpower and kill them. This reveals the place where all that is written in the Holy Scriptures will come to their fulfilment, because their bodies will lie down in the public squared of the great city—which is figuratively called Sodom and Egypt—where also our Lord was crucified, this is the city of Jerusalem.

For three days and one night the great multitude that no one could count, will be taken from every people, tribe, language and nation, before the great day of the Lord, they will gaze on their bodies and refused them to be burial, so that the Holy Scriptures shall be fulfilled. The inhabitants of the earth are also the fourth horse with its rider, they will gloat over them and will celebrate the death of these two prophets, because the two prophets had tormented those who live on the earth, but just like it's written by the apostle Paul speaking about this event, in the first book of Thessalonians chapter five verses two and three:

*"for you know very well that <u>the day of the Lord will come like
a thief in the night.</u> While people are saying, "Peace and safety,"
destruction will come on them suddenly, as labor pains on a
pregnant woman, and they will not escape."*

The fulfilment of the three days and one night, and about the two
witnesses of God, is a prophesy that will have its fulfilment in the
appointed place, in the city of Jerusalem and it concerns the appointed
time of deliverance of God's holy people, for what will be is coming near.

Revelation 10: [9] **For three and a half days** *some from every people, tribe,
language and nation will gaze on their bodies and refuse them burial.* [10] *The
inhabitants of the earth will gloat over them and will celebrate by sending
each other gifts, because these two prophets had tormented those who live on
the earth.*

Then the Lord will come with the clouds of heaven, in the fulfilment of
all prophesies, when the bride goes with her husband, and the fulfilment
of the vision of the son (sons and daughters) sitting at the right hand of
God the Father on his throne which is the sky. And the fulfilment of the
door's temple, open in the sky so the angels enter in the Holy of holies
which is the sky, becoming its eternal pillars. And the fulfilment of the
ark, that is visible over the mount Zion, when the Lord comes for all the
creation that he had done.

Revelation 10:[11] *But after the* **three and a half days the breath** *of life
from God entered them, and they stood on their feet, and terror struck those
who saw them.* [12] *Then they heard a loud voice from heaven saying to them,*
"Come up here." *And they went up to heaven in a cloud, while their
enemies looked on.*

Then, the a great earthquake will occurred at the appointed hour and day,
month and year, this is the end of the 10 days but those days are referred
as the ten of the city based on the great earthquake. And the last seven
days of the creation is referred as the seven thousand people, also based
on the earthquake, is the seven day of creation, Saturday or Sabbath day.

Revelation 10:[13] *At that very hour there was a severe earthquake and **a tenth** of the city collapsed. **Seven** thousand people were killed in the earthquake, and the survivors were terrified and gave glory to the God of heaven.*

The creation of the world have three representations, and the three have everything in common but by faith we understand that the universe was made by God's command, so what we can see is not made of what is visible, this means in creation we are the Lord's work whom he is creating, we couldn't see him but he was right there, for everyone, just as it is written in book of Genesis chapter two verse two:

> **"By the seventh day God had finished the work he had been doing; so on the seventh day he rested from all his work.**"

The Lord of the earth, the creator of mankind and the eternal life for male and female, will finish all creation on the seventh day, because the end was written before its beginning and the beginning is coming to its end. That's the reason why the Holy Scriptures were written in a prophesy, symbolism and spiritual speech, like if everything was already done, and yes was done because God was at the end and even before the beginning. God created its end even with heavenly bodies, and important feasts for signs of time, and not only that, he gave all of him even to the point of to be the word and became in flesh to the world to save us from our own actions and our own plans, he didn't came to be worshiped by all the earth, he proved to be worthy of praise, for he make himself less, so we can be great, and suffer greatly for our sins and evil actions, and defeating death as an action and reaction, and also the one who holds its power, making us victorious by his victory, and eternal, by his love, Amen!

THE SIGN OF THE 70 DAYS

"Daniel and Isaiah"

Ten days are prophetic referred in all the books of the Holy Scriptures, but each book have its own representation with the 10 days, meaning the end of days.

Daniel 9:[27] *He will confirm a covenant with **many for one 'seven.'**...*

Isaiah 6: [2] *Above him were seraphim, each with **six** wings: With **two** wings they covered their faces, with **two** they covered their feet, and with **two** they were flying.*

In the book of the prophet Daniel, the ten days are referred as the sign of the 70 days, but in the 70 days only counts the 62 day. The 62 day is the end of one week those are 7 days. And it's called **"One 7 and 62 sevens"**.

						62 day
1	2	3	4	5	6	7

Daniel 9: [26] ***After the sixty-two 'sevens,'*** *the Anointed One will be put to death and will have nothing.*

After the 62 day is the middle of the week which is on Wednesday. It's called "**The middle of the seven**". In the book of Daniel is mentioned the prince of the holy covenant also is mentioned the ruler who will make a covenant with many on the 62 day also known as **"one seven"** that is one week.

But after the 62 day, he will act deceitfully and will break the covenant that he made with many for one seven, in the middle of the seven, the prince of the holy covenant will be put to death, and the ruler's people will destroy the temple, until the end that is decreed is poured out on him.

Daniel 11: [21] *"He will be succeeded by a contemptible person who has not been given the honor of royalty. He will invade the kingdom when its people feel secure, and he will seize it through intrigue.* [22] *Then an overwhelming army will be swept away before him; both it and a prince of the covenant will be destroyed.* [23] *After coming to an agreement with him, he will act deceitfully, and with only a few people he will rise to power.* [24] *When the richest provinces feel secure, he will invade them…*

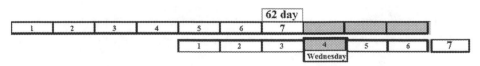

Daniel 9: **In the middle of the 'seven'** *he will put an end to sacrifice and offering.*

Isaiah 7: [8] *... Within* **sixty-five** *years, Ephraim will be too shattered to be a people.*

Now in the sequence of the 70 days, from the 62 day to the 65 day is also written in the book of the prophet Isaiah as 65 years.

The 65 day means "Emmanuel" and "God is with us", the 65 day is found on Friday. The Friday is the last day of the ten days, and that's the end of the sequence referring to the sign of the 70 days. The 70 days it's just a representation of the last days but the 70 doesn't count on the sequence of the 62 day and the 65 day.

It's the sign of an important event and the signs does follows the event chronologically, its sequence is counted by five days. Not counting Sunday or Sabbath day, because its representation is not about creation, it is about a sign of the last week of the age.

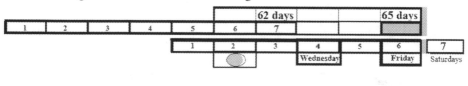

CHAPTER 11

THE 3RD WOE!-THE GREAT EARTHQUAKE

The seven trumpets doesn't have an order in a chronological sequence, but the order is separated in four phases, the third one is called "**The third woe!**" keeping in mind this order it won't be difficult to understand the seven trumpets.

*Revelation 11:[14] The second woe has passed; **the third woe is coming soon.***

Ten days	Three days and a half	The hour	The wrath of the Lamb
First woe!	Second Woe!	Third woe!	A third
5th Trumpet	6th Trumpet	7th Trumpet	Four Trumpets

The third woe! Occurs when the Lord comes for his holy people and the holy people shall be in the sky and with the Lord, while their enemies looked on. And the voices in heaven are The Lord's Holy people with their crown of life standing with the Lord in heaven, they were proclaiming the Lord's reign. It's called the kingdom of the Lord and the Kingdom of his Messiah, keeping in mind that Jesus is the Lord, both "**Lord and Messiah**". All the Holy Scriptures, are sealed in this way, but Jesus is the Lamb.

Revelation 11:[15] The seventh angel sounded his trumpet, and there were loud voices in heaven, which said:

"The kingdom of the world has become
the kingdom of our Lord and of his Messiah,
and he will reign for ever and ever."

The twenty-four thrones, the twenty-four elders and the twenty-four crowns refer the Lord's victory on Sunday 24. But those twenty-four elders represent the sum of the 12 apostles of the Lamb plus the 12 tribes of Judea (thrones) plus 12 apostles of the Lamb (elders) equals the 24 (crowns of life) because it is written in the book of the apostle Luke:

Luke 22: [29] *And I confer on you a kingdom, just as my Father conferred one on me,* [30] ***so that you may eat and drink at my table in my kingdom and sit on thrones, judging the twelve tribes of Israel.***

Also when Jesus says "…**so that you may eat and drink on my table in my kingdom…**" is also representing the Great blanket and the fulfilment of all judgment also at the last day of creation, this whole important event will take place in heaven, and so the Kings with their crowns of life will acknowledge the King of kings.

Revelation 11: [16] *And the twenty-four elders, who were seated on their thrones before God, fell on their faces and worshiped God…*

And because the whole important event will take place after resurrection, then the Holy of holies places, which is the sky, at Jesus' coming in the sky, is the fulfilment of God's temple in heaven that in visions the temple appears open in the sky, is because the temple is his body and his crown is his glory as the eternal God, and because the door of the temple was opened in heaven, is referring the ark of his covenant in heaven, both visions fulfilled as well.

Revelation 11: [19] *Then* ***God's temple in heaven was opened, and within his temple was seen the ark of his covenant.*** *And there came flashes of lightning, rumblings, peals of thunder,* ***an earthquake…***

After the fulfilment of the Lord's temple in heaven at his coming, the great earthquake will occurred at the same hour of God's coming and the four angels released to killed all mankind, this is called, "**The wrath of the Lamb**".

And the seven trumpets have an order of four phases, the first event is represented in the fifth trumpet, the second event is represented in the sixth trumpet, and the third event is represented in the seventh trumpet.

But the fourth and last event is called "**The wrath of the Lamb**" because he is Lord of lords and King of Kings, the wrath is represented in the four trumpets, it's the fourth event and its part of the three woes! But because is the last event, is called "**a third**" and refer total destruction over the earth, but like a seal.

After Jesus's coming and at the same hour shall be a severe earthquake, then the wrath of the Lamb shall be first with a severe hailstorm severe because from the sky huge hailstones, each weighing about a hundred pounds, will fall on people.

Revelation 11:[19]*… and **a severe hailstorm.***

THE WRATH OF THE LAMB
"THE 1/3RD"

The wrath of the Lamb is God's judgment over the earth, when its written, "A third of the earth" refer all the earth. "A third" just represent the real chronologic order of the seven trumpets. And the first trumpet refer the judgment over the earth, the sever hailstorm is the cause of fire, because the hailstones fell on the flammable material, and also the cause of blood, because from the sky the huge hailstones, each weighing about a hundred pounds, will fall on people, the prophesy always will be written as done, because it will be.

Revelation 8:[7] *The first angel sounded his trumpet, and there came hail and fire mixed with blood, and it was hurled down on the earth. **A third** of the earth was burned up, **a third** of the trees were burned up, and all the green grass was burned up.*

In the second trumpet refer the judgment over the mountains and the seas because of the water increase over the earth. And when is written, "A third of the leaving creatures in the sea die" refer all the leaving creatures in the sea will die. And when it's written "A third of the ships were destroyed" refer that all the ships were destroyed.

Revelation 8:[8] *The second angel sounded his trumpet, and something like a huge mountain, all ablaze, was thrown into the sea.* ***A third*** *of the sea turned into blood,* [9] ***a third*** *of the living creatures in the sea died, and* ***a third*** *of the ships were destroyed.*

The third trumpet refer the judgment over the rivers and the springs of living water, by the falling of a great star of sulfur to cause such a devastation over sweet waters. The star is written literally because the facts of the aspects already mentioned, because in the four trumpets is not found the symbolic pronounced.

Revelation 8:[10] *The third angel sounded his trumpet, and a great star, blazing like a torch, fell from the sky on* ***a third*** *of the rivers and on the springs of water—* [11] *the name of the star is Wormwood.* ***A third*** *of the waters turned bitter, and many people died from the waters that had become bitter.*

The fourth trumpet refer the judgment over the earth by the heavenly bodies, the heavenly bodies are signs for the years, months, days and hours, but when those are lost, even the level in life over the earth is lost, clouds covers the surface of the earth like never before, and the darkness becomes complete on the earth, because of the changes of the four winds of heaven, the elements over the earth having whole new positions, and a new heaven will be found after that.

Revelation 8:[12] *The fourth angel sounded his trumpet, and* ***a third*** *of the sun was struck,* ***a third*** *of the moon, and* ***a third*** *of the stars, so that* ***a third*** *of them turned dark.* ***A third*** *of the day was without light, and also* ***a third*** *of the night.*

This is called, "The wrath of the Lamb" it's written as **a third** of mankind but the meaning is the four first trumpets as "**A third**" and represents total destruction but only as a judgment over the earth. The wrath of the Lamb is the whole judgment for all mankind, this occurs when God commends to release the four angels that are bound at the great river Euphrates, this refer the new year and its first month, also the day and the hour is found. This is before it happens, and refer when it happens at his presence.

Revelation 9: [15] *And the four angels who had been kept ready for this very hour and day and month and year were released to kill* ***a third*** *of mankind.*

CHAPTER 12

THE HOLY CITY-SUNDAY 24

There is so many interpretations for the rod of gold and, in the book of Isaiah chapter six verse six, it's called like a live coal, which a seraphim had taken with tongs from the altar. Remember that this repeats in the prophetic speech, what he have in his hands, its a little scroll open, but in the book of Isaiah it's represented like a live coal from the altar which refer the earth. In the book of Ezekiel chapter two verse nine, is repeated as a scroll from the angel's hand, remember that prophetically its reveal in a vision, also in the book of Ezekiel chapter three verse three, explains that the scroll have to be eaten and in the mouth is sweet as honey, but in the book of Revelation chapter ten verse two is repeat how the angel have the little scroll open in his hand and that the scroll is no more sealed, there in the chapter ten verse eight explains how God's voice commands his servants to take the little book from the angels' hand, and in verse nine explains how the servants of God took the scroll and when they have eating the scroll means that they read and understand the Holy Scriptures, then in verse ten explains how the words of the scroll sound sweet as they speak, this is explained in the book of Jeremiah chapter 15 verse 16:

"¹⁶ *When your words came, I ate them;*
they were my joy and my heart's delight,
for I bear your name,
*L*ord *God Almighty.*"

In the book of Revelation chapter ten verse eleven, its explained how God command his servants to prophesy again about many peoples, nations, languages and kings, then in the book of Revelation chapter eleven verse one, explains the little scroll, but like a rod to measure the city, the altar and its worshipers. In the book of Revelation chapter twenty-one, verse fifteen, repeats the little scroll like a measuring rod with the prophetic meaning of "12" to measure the city, its gates and its doors, but the whole meaning of this refers a little book that laid open in the angels' hand, this angel is the same that have the seal of the living God.

Revelation 21:⁹ One of the seven angels who had the seven bowls full of the seven last plagues came and said to me, **"Come, I will show you the bride, the wife of the Lamb."**

The way the angel shows to the servants of God the Holy City is through the little scroll that laid open in the angel's hand, this little book is figuratively called "the measuring rod" there is only three phases to measure; the Holy city, its gates and its doors. The Holy city has a different point of view apart of the seals and the trumpets.

Revelation 22:¹⁵ The angel who talked with me had a measuring rod of gold to measure **the city**, *its* **gates** *and its* **walls.**

THE HOLY CITY

First the Holy city. It explains how the Holy City was laid like a square, and also gives the sign of his measurement, those are; 12 (golden rod) x 12,000 (stadia) = 144,000 (Holy City). It is written that the Holy city was laid like a squared, because of the golden rod on the three phases, counting the gates of the great wall and the doors, part of the measurements of the Holy City.

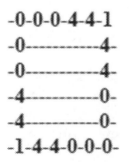

Revelation 21:[16] **The city was laid out like a square,** *as long as it was wide. He measured the city with the rod and found it to be 12,000 stadia in length, and as **wide** and **high** as it is **long.***

The way is measured the Holy City is referred in the book of Genesis as the measurement of the ark of the covenant, symbolically it doesn't count the measurements, what it counts is the way its measured by Noah, because Noah did built the ark as it is written by God's command as a mystery on the creation of the world this is found to be fulfilled before the prophetic flood of 150 days or 5 months which are 10 days of war before the end.

Genesis 6:[15] *This is how you are about to build it: The ark is to be 300 cubits **long,** 50 cubits **wide** and 30 cubits **high.***

IT'S WALL

Just like the Holy City was laid like a squared, so the high wall, it just explains the squared using the four winds of heaven, and in that way the squared is found with the twelve gates divided by four because of the squared meaning, and it's found to be four walls as well;

Revelation 21:[13] *There were three gates* **on the east,** *three* **on the north,** *three* **on the south** *and three* **on the west.**

3 doors to the north

3 doors to the west   -4-4-1-   **3 doors** to the east
-4----4-
-1-4-4-

3 doors to the south

Remember that the measuring rod is "twelve", but the wall have also twelve in so many representations which are the same, the twelve gates of the high wall and the twelve angels at the twelve gates and also the twelve names of the apostles of the Lamb written on the gates refer only one meaning"12" and it's found to be measured the high wall like these; 12 (the measuring rod) x 12 (gates) = 144 (high wall).

*Revelation 21:[17] The angel measured the wall using human measurement, and it was **144** cubits thick.*

IT'S GATES

Now the doors. The sign of the doors of the Holy City are very important at this point, because in the spiritual speech we inter the Holy City through the gates, but its meaning is easy to understand. The measuring rod is "12" and the Holy City have a high wall and the high wall have twelve foundations also are twelve doors and each gate is made of a single pearl, and its final measurement is this; 12 (the measuring rod) + 12 (Pearls) = 24 (gates)

Revelation 21:[21] The twelve gates were twelve pearls, each gate made of a single pearl...

```
-0-0-0-4-4-1-
-0-----4-2-4- =It's gates
-0-----1-4-4- =It's walls
-4----------0-
-4----------0-
-1-4-4-0-0-0- =The holy city
```

Now after the measured wall and the measured Holy City and Its gates, is found the 24, this prophetically refer the day when Jesus rose early on Sunday also known as the first day of creation because was a day of the first day of the week, the day of the Lord's victory over death, and prophetically the temple refer Jesus' body and at the third day Jesus rebuilt the temple as he prophesy to the Jews in front of the temple of Jerusalem when they didn't understand that jesus was talking about his body, this is the reason why the temple is not in the city as the Holy Scriptures refer is because the temple rose on Sunday early in the morning and departed to his throne which is the sky, he is the only way, like the great street of pure gold of the Holy City;

Revelation 21:[21] ...The great street of the city was of gold, as pure as transparent glass.[22] I did not see a temple in the city, **because the Lord God Almighty and the Lamb are its temple.**

Jesus' victory was on Sunday, the 24th day, this is the prophesy about the nations and the book of the Lamb is referring the creation, which fulfills every day since the Lord's victory and will be concluded until the last day of creation or the end of the age:

Revelation 21:[27] *Nothing impure will ever enter it, nor will anyone who does what is shameful or deceitful,* **but only those whose names are written in the Lamb's book of life.**

THE HOLY CITY- SUNDAY 24 SATURDAY

The fulfilment of the Seal of the leaving God is the understanding of the first day of creation and Sunday is the first day of creation, in this we acknowledge who is our heavenly father, this fulfilment repeats several times in this little book, because the understanding and the acknowledge of creation is starting disclosing the first day of creation, and why is the first day of creation? Is because of Jesus' victory over flesh on Sunday 24, the first day of the week and also the first day of the creation, disclosing the last day of creation as well, why the last day of creation? because the first day of creation was the first day of the week on Jesus' victory over flesh, so the last day of the week and the last day of creation shall be on Saturday figuratively called **"Sabbath day"** because on that day The Lord rested from all his work of creating that he had done. Which means that day was all creation concluded and God will be in the city as it is written in the book of Revelation:

Revelation 22:[3] *No longer will there be any curse.* **The throne of God and of the Lamb will be in the city, and his servants will serve him.** [4] **They will see his face, and his name will be on their foreheads.**

Chapter 13

THE SEVEN LETTERS OF GOD

THE SEVEN LETTERS

The seven letters open to the seven continents. In the seven letters our savior Jesus Christ is speaking about himself as a second or third person, <u>this starts at the beginning</u> in each one of the seven letters <u>and at the end</u> of each one of the seven letters, this is why he says: "I am the **Alfa** and the **Omega**" The letter **"A"** and the letter **"Z"** of the alphabet. This means that in each of the seven letters any second or third person are just the representation of our **Lord Jesus Christ.** This repeats on the seven letters in the presentation of its individual message, and at the conclusion of each one of them. **This letters are written up for the bride of the Lamb, and the Bride is the Church of God in the seven continents.**

"The messengers give the message, and the message of each letter is for the churches of God in each one of the seven continents, and because its based on the prophetic reference in the book of revelation, the testimony of things to come, and the fulfilment of all prophesy is near with the elects, who also give testimony of what is near and the signs that follows this important event."

Revelation 2: [20] *The mystery of the seven stars that you saw in my right hand and of the seven golden lampstands is this:* ***The seven stars are the angels of the seven churches, and the seven lampstands are the seven churches.***

Search for the message, and you will find it, the seven letters are open because is time to revealed them.

SOUTH AMERICA

- ➤ **Ephesus** means: **South America.**
- ➤ **Lampstand** means: it's **Church. (Continent)**
- ➤ **Star** means: **The messenger or Angel.**
- ➤ **Our repentance is God's forgiveness of sins.**
- ➤ **His Name** is: **Jesus Christ of Nazareth.**
- ➤ **Jesus Christ** is: our **First Love (The First and the Last.)**
- ➤ **The Holy Spirit** is: **Jesus Christ.**
- ➤ **Victor's Crown** means: **Eternal Life.**
- ➤ The Tree of Life is **"Jesus Christ"** and the paradise of God is **"The Sky"** He does represent Life and **also our resurrection Day".**

Revelation 2:[1] *"To **the angel** of the church in **Ephesus** write:*

AFRICA

- ➤ **Smyrna** means: **Africa.**
- ➤ **Lampstand** means: it's **Church. (Continent)**
- ➤ **Star** means: **The messenger or the angel.**
- ➤ **The first and Last** means: Sunday and Sabbath.
- ➤ **Weak people** means: **Liars.**
- ➤ **Satan** means also: **The devil, the ancient serpent.**
- ➤ **Victor's Crown** means: **Eternal Life.**
- ➤ **The great war of 10 Days before Jesus' coming.**

Revelation 2:[8] *"To **the angel** of **the church** in **Smyrna** write:*

ASIA

- ➤ **Pergamum** means: **Asia**
- ➤ **Lampstand** means: it's **Church. (Continent)**
- ➤ **Star** means: **The messenger or the angel.**
- ➤ **The sword of God** is: **The Word of God.**
- ➤ **His Name** is: **Jesus Christ of Nazareth.**
- ➤ **Antipas** refer: **Jesus,** The Christ of God. (The faithful witness.)
- ➤ **Satan** means: **The red Dragon.**
- ➤ **That city** means: **Jerusalem.**

THE HARP OF GOD 24

- ➤ **The White Stone with** a new name written on it is: **24**th **day.**
- ➤ **Victor's Crown** means: **Eternal Life.**

Revelation 2:[12] *"To **the angel** of **the church** in **Pergamum** write:*

EUROPE

- ➤ **Thyatira** means: **Europe.**
- ➤ **Lampstand** means: it's **Church. (Continent)**
- ➤ **Star** means: **The messenger or Angel.**
- ➤ **The Son of God** is: **Jesus, The Christ of God.**
- ➤ **At First** means: **In the beginning.**
- ➤ **That Woman Jezebel** means: **Jerusalem.**
- ➤ **Bed of suffering** means: **The great flood (internationally)**
- ➤ **At first** means: From **the beginning and Jesus' victory on Sunday.**
- ➤ **Lampstand** means: it's **Church.** (Continent).
- ➤ **Repentance** leads to salvation
- ➤ **Sexual immorality** means: **Adulterers** also means **Idolaters.**
- ➤ **Morning Star** means: **The Lord Jesus Christ' presence.**
- ➤ **Hold on to what you have** As: **The Word of God.**
- ➤ **The one who searches Hearts and Minds** is: **The Lord Himself.**
- ➤ **Victor's Crown** means: **Eternal Life.**

Revelation 3:[18] *"To **the angel** of **the church** in **Thyatira** write:*

ANTARTIC

- ➤ **Sardis** means: **Antarctica.**
- ➤ **Star** means: **The messenger or Angel.**
- ➤ **Lampstand** means: it's **Church. (Continent)**
- ➤ **Repentance** and baptism in the name of **Jesus Christ of Nazareth is: salvation.**
- ➤ **White clothes refer the righteous acts of the saints.**
- ➤ **What you have received and heard** That is: **"The Word of God".**
- ➤ **Victor's Crown** means: **Eternal Life.**
- ➤ **The book of life** refers to: **Jesus Christ himself.**

Revelation 3:[1] *"To* **the angel** *of* **the church** *in* **Sardis** *write:*

NORTH AMERICA

- ➢ **Philadelphia** means: **North America.**
- ➢ **Lampstand** means: it's **Church (Continent)**
- ➢ **Liar** means: those who are of **the synagogue of Satan.**
- ➢ **Star** means: **The messenger "The Angel".**
- ➢ **The first and Last** means: **Sunday and Sabbath**
- ➢ *David* and is: **The Messenger of Philadelphia**
- ➢ **Our repentance is God's forgiveness of sins.**
- ➢ **The key of David to open the door of the temple of the Lord is: the 24**[th] **day.**
- ➢ **Victor's Crown** means: **Eternal Life.**
- ➢ **The pillars of the Temple of God** are the ones who maintain the testimony of Jesus.

The two pillars refer **the testimony of Jesus**, the final testimony are three days and a half to be prepared, this refer Jesus' coming.

Revelation 3:[7] *"To* **the angel** *of* **the church** *in* **Philadelphia** *write:*

AUSTRALIA

- ➢ **Laodicea** means: **Australia.**
- ➢ **Lampstand** means: it's **Church. (Continent)**
- ➢ **The Amen** refer **Jesus Christ of Nazareth.**
- ➢ **The Faithful and true witness** is: **Jesus Christ of Nazareth.**
- ➢ **Hot or Cold** means: **Good or Evil.**
- ➢ **Victor's Crown** means: **Eternal Life.**
- ➢ **Our repentance is God's forgiveness of sins.**

Be earnest and repent Means: **Hear and open The Door of the temple.**

> **"I will spit you out of my mouth-salve so you can see"**
> **"Those whom I love I rebuke and discipline"**

Revelation 3:[14] *"To* **the angel** *of* **the church** *in* **Laodicea** *write:*

Now there is nothing left for me to say, but I will be with you, until you finally defeat fear, even away I still will be with you, this is the little scroll and the reason why I am spiritually born, I expect you to understand and all your questions be answered, when our testimony is finish that is going to be important, but until then, I want you to be glad, and to smiled, because I know a great God, he showed to me how great he is, and how much he loves all of you, I just can fail him, so I am here, with you, because of him, I myself was in trouble, but I understood that there is a time to cry and there is time to smiled, even though I was in trouble by understanding I stand, not just for me, but for you too, but I knew who sent me, and I know who is the truth. I don't want you to be afraid, I want you to be stronger, and with all your heart hold on to his promises, because he will come and everything will be changed to immortality, understand that this concerns your happiness, and that is all I want for you, hope to see you and to speak to you, but first you must be strong, and understand, that you have a great God, and I believed that he will take care of all of you and me, for eternity, you must be prepared for this will come you want it or not, prepared or not, happy or sad. But I will be here enough time to show you this way, you know the way to home, Jesus is the way, the true and life.

There shall be no pain in your heart, you will be ok! Just don't give up praying, for your family, for your friends and for me, in the name of the Lord God almighty, I encourage you to be glad and lift up your hands, for the imperfection will become perfect, and our savior is near at the door. And the door is open.

And as a servant of God, I will finish our testimony having God as my witness as well for I did not sent myself, I am with you as well. Tell the church for me, that I sent to them my spirit as words to blessed them, and tell them that I care about them enough to be thankful by the way they encouraged me to walk on in this life, "1rst Corinthians chapter 13" God blessed all of you, and don't give up, you are the reason why I stand, even until the end. Let me lift up my hands too, and be glad that my savior will give me the crown of life to be with you wherever he goes, and also to see you smiling that is what really makes my life eternal, to me, it is all I desired.

Glory be to God Almighty, Halleluiah, and Halleluiah! The Lord Reigns, Glory and honor and thanks and power and victory be to our God and only Savior, the worthy, the God of love, Amen!

Revelation 22:[20] He who testifies to these things says, **"Yes, I am coming soon."**

Amen. Come, Lord Jesus.

[21] The grace of the Lord Jesus be with God's people. Amen.